Okinawa

Two rice-straw ropes (a male and a female) engage in a titanic tug of war (*tsunahiki*) during a festival of the sixth lunar month. Victory by the female rope (*above*) portends a bountiful rice harvest.

THIS BEAUTIFUL WORLD　　VOL. 41

Okinawa

by CLAYTON L. HOGG

 KODANSHA INTERNATIONAL LTD.
TOKYO, NEW YORK & SAN FRANCISCO

Distributors:
UNITED STATES: *Harper & Row, Publishers, Inc., 10 East 53rd Street, New York, New York 10022.* SOUTH AMERICA: *Harper & Row, International Department.* CANADA: *Fitzhenry & Whiteside Limited, 150 Lesmill Road, Don Mills, Ontario.* MEXICO AND CENTRAL AMERICA: *HARLA S. A. de C. V., Apartado 30–546, Mexico 4, D. F.* BRITISH COMMONWEALTH *(excluding Canada and the Far East)*: *TABS, 7 Maiden Lane, London WC2.* EUROPE: *Boxerbooks Inc., Limmatstrasse 111, 8031 Zurich.* AUSTRALIA AND NEW ZEALAND: *Book Wise (Australia) Pty. Ltd., 104–8 Sussex Street, Sydney.* THAILAND: *Central Department Store Ltd., 306 Silom Road, Bangkok.* HONG KONG AND SINGAPORE: *Books for Asia Ltd., 30 Tat Chee Avenue, Kowloon; 65 Crescent Road, Singapore 15.* THE FAR EAST: *Japan Publications Trading Company, P.O. Box 5030, Tokyo International, Tokyo.*

Published by Kodansha International Ltd., 2-12-21 Otowa, Bunkyo-ku, Tokyo 112 and Kodansha International/USA, Ltd., 10 East 53rd Street, New York, New York 10022 and 44 Montgomery Street, San Francisco, California 94104. Copyright in Japan 1973 by Kodansha International Ltd. All rights reserved. Printed in Japan.

LCC 72-93532
ISBN 0-87011-189-2
JBC 0025-783684-2361

First edition, 1973
Second printing, 1975

Contents

Isles of Courtesy 7
Isles of Festivity 51
Map of Ryukyus 55
Map of Okinawa 62
Isles of Diplomacy 91

Isles of Courtesy

On the fifteenth day of May, 1972, the Ryukyu Islands, including Okinawa, reverted to Japan. "Rarely in the history of relations between two countries," wrote Robert S. Ingersoll, the United States ambassador in Tokyo, "has there been such a day as this one, when one country peacefully returns to another country territories it gained from a tragic war." It was the beginning of a short statement written by the American envoy for a special May 15 supplement of *The Japan Times*. In that same edition, Prime Minister Eisaku Sato wrote: "On behalf of the entire Japanese people, I wish to express my sincere gratification that Okinawa has been returned to the homeland...." For Sato it was the climax of his career; he was soon, having signed the reversion agreement, to step down from the highest elective office in the country.

Millions of people on both sides of the Pacific, watching the ceremonial signing of the treaty on a split screen through satellite television, saw the president of the United States in Washington and the prime minister of Japan in Tokyo simultaneously put their signatures to the agreement. Then a good many Americans trotted dutifully to their encyclopedias and their atlases to look up the Ryukyus. Where exactly were they? Somewhere in the Pacific, to

OKINAWA

be sure, everyone knew that; but even many who had been living in June, 1945, had in twenty-seven frantic postwar years pretty much forgotten about what Sato called "the bloodiest battlefield" of the Second World War, and many who watched the ceremony had not even been born when the battle for Okinawa was fought. The Japanese, on the other side of the ocean, had no need to refer to maps: they were entirely familiar with the location of the Ryukyus, a former prefecture that was now once again to regain that status.

Geographically, the Ryukyus include all the islands, of which the largest and most important is Okinawa, in the 780-mile arc between southern Kyushu and Taiwan. Politically and historically, the definition is somewhat different and has tended to be more variable. In 1609, for example, a military expedition from Satsuma, in southern Kyushu, invaded the Ryukyus and claimed all the islands north of Okinawa as an integral part of Japan. Then, 270 years later, Japan annexed Okinawa and the southern Ryukyus, making a prefecture of the entire chain. After the Pacific war ended, the United States separated "some exterior regions from Japan for political and administrative purposes." In April, 1952, under the terms of the San Francisco Peace Treaty, the United States became the administrative authority for all the Ryukyus south of latitude 29° North. Then, on December 25, 1953, the Amami Islands (north of the twenty-seventh parallel) were returned to Japan, which left the political delineation of the Ryukyus much the same as it had been following the Satsuma invasion of 1609.

Included are seventy-three islands, of which forty-seven are permanently inhabited. Some 87 percent of the Ryukyuan population of nearly a million live in the Okinawan group; the two other main groups are Miyako and Yaeyama. These are the islands and the

ISLES OF COURTESY

people that I propose to write about here, having spent several years during the American occupation teaching English in an Okinawan school and travelling, when I had the time, not only across the big island but also to many more remote islands.

I cannot help wondering what effect reversion to the prospering homeland is destined to have upon Okinawans. Will it change still further their age-old ways, their well-developed ability to make the best of a bad situation? For many centuries, throughout their recorded history and long before, Ryukyuans have found themselves straddling a fence, peering anxiously for a time in one direction, then in the other. Until the late nineteenth century those two directions were Japan and China; after the end of the Pacific war, it was Japan and the United States that claimed the islanders' divided attention. Through all those centuries of accepting conditions they were powerless to alter, Ryukyuans have learned to face an unhappy, even a desperate situation with a smile, and with an adroitness that has gone a long way to disarm their invaders. And as the invaders have come and gone, Ryukyuans have never forgotten their ancient folk songs and dances, their own customs and religion, their hearty pleasure in a bang-up party with plenty to eat for everyone and plenty to drink for the men.

Learning to like a people so gallant and insouciant is, I found, one of the easiest things in the world. From my point of view, Ryukyuans have a happy talent for relaxing, for taking it easy, for keeping their cool. This may be only a defense mechanism to help them survive the extended and sultry Ryukyuan summers, but it works. Long ago, the islands were called "the land of the happy immortals," and an inscription on a bell from the old Shuri Castle speaks of the Ryukyus as the islands of eternal youth. I think I

OKINAWA

discovered how the islanders gained this enviable reputation: it arises from a combination of their easy-going attitude toward the vicissitudes of life and their admirable ability to extract the maximum pleasure from either work or play. They even speak of of "Ryukyuan time" as though it were a special kind of horology that had little to do with the more precise and exigent time kept in other parts of the world.

The islands may be lacking in spectacular tourist attractions, such as famous old buildings, great cities, majestic mountains, but there are compensations aplenty. A not inconsiderable one is the fact that the air is breathable: it is so pure, indeed, that one may still watch the sun setting in the East China Sea. No filthy sky snuffs it out as it descends toward the evening horizon. And although Ryukyuan scenery is not overwhelming, it is extremely pleasant and human: coastal highways weave along white beaches that jut in and out of smiling green hills; offshore coral rocks, sculptured by the waves, frame distant blue islands.

At the same time, the blandness of the Ryukyus is touched with spice, with a bit of wildness to temper the tameness and keep a man on his toes. Twenty-four uninhabited islands are entirely given over to untouched nature, and some of the smaller inhabited islands are only partly humanized. Iriomote, for example, one of the two large islands in the Yaeyamas, has a population of only two thousand huddled along the narrow coasts, while the heavily forested, mountainous interior is virtually untouched. Even Okinawa itself, as veterans of that "bloody battlefield" will recall, is far from tamed: in the south, unkempt hills are covered with a tall, shaggy-headed grass (*Miscanthus sinensis*), which somewhat resembles the pampas grass of South America, and the fernlike cycad, while the north of

ISLES OF COURTESY

Okinawa remains a mountainous forest.

Nor is the Ryukyuan animal kingdom altogether domesticated. There are at least twenty-nine varieties of snakes, of which five that live on land are poisonous; the deadliest is the *habu,* a pit viper whose bite, if not treated promptly with first aid and serum, is almost inevitably fatal. The *habu* is a night feeder and is found everywhere in the Ryukyus except on such flat islands as Miyako. The sea has its hazards too: stings of jellyfish, stonefish, and turkeyfish require emergency treatment; the tail of the stingray may inflict a serious cut, carrying with it enough poison to make its victim violently ill; seven of the sea snakes, although usually non-aggressive, also go armed with a highly toxic venom; the sea urchin, lying everywhere on the reefs, has spines that may cause an extremely disagreeable infection; the very pretty coneshells found on the beaches carry barbs of death; and even the coral itself can be poisonous. The list of Ryukyuan animal hazards may sound formidable, but the fact remains that millions of islanders and tourists wander freely across the land and spend hours in the fabulous underwater gardens of the sea without ever coming to harm.

Ryukyuan weather too may turn suddenly wild when a typhoon strikes. Although the islands are seldom hit more than once or twice a year during the typhoon season (between May and December), destruction can be extensive, particularly if there has been little prior warning and particularly on the low islands. At the same time, typhoons are not an unmitigated disaster. During times of drought, when the water supply dries up and crops are endangered, community priestesses pray for a typhoon; then, if the prayers are answered, the people take time off and catch up on their sleep. Foreigners have developed their own way of coping: they give, or

OKINAWA 🏯

go to, typhoon parties, where there is plenty of liquor to take a man's mind off the roaring winds and the torrential rains.

The subject of wild life brings to mind nocturnal amusements. In Okinawa, today, there are three main areas given over almost exclusively to bars and patronized largely, at least in the past, by American servicemen. Two of these amusement centers, Kin and Koza, came with the occupation, but one, Tsuji, was set aside as a licensed quarter as long ago as 1672. At the turn of the century it was estimated that there were some twenty-eight hundred prostitutes in Naha, although "prostitute" is perhaps an unfortunate word to use here. In Okinawa now, as in old Japan, the profession carries with it none of the connotations of guilt and shame that it has for Western ears: it is a métier like any other and one that, for an unlettered girl, pays better than most.

For me, another attractive quality about Okinawa is its happy blend of old and new, an amalgam that is still well balanced and that I can only hope will stay that way. There are glittering American-style drive-in restaurants, but there are also plenty of small eating-houses given over to Chinese and Japanese as well as Okinawan food. There are smooth American-built highways and there are bumpy country roads. There are supermarkets and there are little neighborhood shops kept in the front room of the shopkeeper's house. A part-time farmer may drive his shiny new car to his postage-stamp-sized field, where he will till the soil in the same way his Stone Age ancestors did.

Okinawa, as an ancient target for investigation from the more powerful kingdoms of Japan and China, has through most of its life been a blend of the old and the new, the indigenous and the imported. All too often it has been the importation that has won

⛩ ISLES OF COURTESY

out. Take the very name of the island, for example. Okinawans have always called it Uchina, but no one else has ever paid the slightest attention to what Okinawans call their island. The Chinese gave the chain the name Liu Ch'iu, which has been romanized in sixty different forms and Japanized as Ryūkyū. Okinawa, the name bestowed on Uchina by the Japanese, may be translated as "rope in the offing." The ancient Chinese and Japanese may have viewed the islands as floating in the sea, but they are in fact firmly anchored to the ocean floor, for they are the peaks of a high range of largely submerged mountains. Standing on an Okinawan hill, I find it difficult to realize that I am atop a mountain twice as high as Mt. Fuji, but it is true enough: the Ryukyu Trench, southeast of Okinawa, has been sounded to a depth of 24,629 feet.

To the west flows the Kuroshio ("the black current," more familiarly known as "the Japan current"), a river within the ocean that enters the East China Sea between Taiwan and Yonaguni and moves in a northeasterly direction at a speed of about fifty miles a day. The importance of the Kuroshio to the Ryukyus can hardly be overestimated, for in addition to bringing with it an abundance of marine life, it ensures agreeably warm water the year around which in turn makes for a generally temperate winter climate. In Naha the average low in January, the coldest month, is 55° Fahrenheit, the average high 66°. The lowest winter temperature ever recorded at Naha is 44°.

Summers, on the other hand, tend to be swelteringly hot, with temperatures approaching 90° and a relative humidity averaging 80 percent. In between the two extremes are spring, with long periods of heavy rain, and autumn, when the clear, temperate, cloudless days are marred only by an occasional typhoon. Occasional as it is,

OKINAWA 🎏

however, the typhoon can be a tremendously destructive force that greatly limits the kinds of crops islanders can grow. Sugarcane, the biggest cash crop, will withstand a typhoon that is not a direct hit, and both pineapplies and sweet potatoes also exhibit a strong ability to survive the winds and the rains.

Rice is easily destroyed. It also requires more labor than other crops and brings in a smaller cash return. Moreover, suitable land is extremely limited. Only about 28 percent of Ryukyu land is arable (coming to about one-sixth of an acre per person), and of that only some three percent can be used for wet rice.

This combination of weather conditions and generally poor soil seems to have had a limiting effect on the size of many apparently unrelated objects, from farm plots to people. When communally-held feudal land was redistributed, each farmer was given several small plots in an attempt to make the grants as equal as possible insofar as quality of the soil, danger of drought, proximity to salt water and spray, and exposure to typhoons were concerned. The result has been a patchwork landscape that resembles densely populated and cultivated parts of Europe.

Although possessing, no doubt, a common or similar ethnic background, the Okinawan physical type is quite distinct from that of other Japanese. There is also a close connection between the two languages, although they broke away so long ago (some say about fifteen hundred years) that they are no longer mutually intelligible. The Ryukyuans actually have four distinct tongues, those spoken in the Amami, Okinawa, Miyako, and Yaeyama groups, plus innumerable dialects and subdialects. Nor are all of these mutually intelligible to Ryukyuans themselves. There is, for example, considerable difference between the language heard in the

ISLES OF COURTESY

northern part of Okinawa and that of the south. In recent years, the Naha dialect has become the most widely spoken throughout the islands.

Japanese is the official language, the language taught in the schools, heard over the radio and on television and in movie houses, printed in newspapers, and used by official government agencies, but Ryukyuans still feel more at home in one or another of the familiar dialects of their own language. Consequently, most Okinawans are now bilingual, and some who have had extensive dealings with the occupying forces have become trilingual. As a result of contemporary methods of mass communication, it is to be expected that within the next few generations the local tongues will have given way altogether to standard Japanese.

Language aside, there are many other points of resemblance between the people of the main islands and the Ryukyuans, among them an uncertainty about what to do with the *gaijin*, the "foreigner." In Naha as in Tokyo he will very likely not be invited home, even if there is no insurmountable language barrier; he will probably, if the necessity arises, be entertained in a restaurant.

In this regard, however, perhaps because of my close daily contacts with Okinawans, I was lucky: I was invited to several parties, or celebrations (*iwai*, to use the Japanese word).

One was to mark the opening of a new building where I had taken an apartment. When I arrived and looked in through the front door, I saw only women, all so busy chatting that they were quite unaware of my inquisitive presence. I then went up the outside stairs to the second floor, where I added my shoes to a large jumble of other, obviously male shoes, and went into a large room. At first glance I was bewildered by its size, but then I realized that

OKINAWA 🛕

it was only three ordinary rooms separated by sliding doors and that the doors had been removed for the party.

The three rooms had become a banquet hall so to speak, and the male guests were now sitting on cushions against its walls as the daughters of the new landlord circulated around offering trays of food and filling glasses with whiskey, beer, or *awamori* (distilled rice wine). I was conducted to one of the cushions and as I tucked my legs beneath me, to await the arrival of food and drink, I noticed that the other men, happily drinking and gossiping away, were taking from the food trays offered them only some thin slices of raw fish (*sashimi*). Later, it was explained to me that if a man wants to get the full pleasure out of his liquor, he does not spoil it with cooked food. That comes afterward.

On the trays, along with such Japanese dishes as *sashimi*, pickled vegetables, and sea food and vegetables fried tempura-style, were typically Okinawan foods like fried pork, and sweet potatoes mixed with other vegetables in a thick sauce.

After the guests had had several drinks and had eaten all they wanted, the landlord-host, carrying a bottle of scotch in his hand, moved over—walking, so to speak, on his knees—to the man who had been in charge of the construction of the house, poured out a drink, spoke a few words of thanks, and then offered it to the builder. The latter, after emptying the glass, filled it again and offered it, with a return of compliments, to the landlord. That gentleman promptly drained his drink and then moved on, still on his knees, to the next guest, with whom he exchanged similar drinks and compliments; the process was repeated with all the men who had had charge of various aspects of the building.

When, at length, my host reached me, he filled my glass, thanked

ISLES OF COURTESY

me for becoming his tenant, and expressed the hope that we would always have a happy relationship. Having drunk, I filled the glass, handed it to him, and enunciated, as well as I could, a similar hope for a happy future. I was beginning to feel the liquor a bit when I saw, somewhat to my horror, that the builder now had a bottle in his hand and had begun moving down the line, exchanging drinks and compliments with each man, just as the new landlord had done. The builder was followed by the second man in line, then by the third, and so it went. By this time the room seemed to have become considerably noisier than it had been at the start, and (for me at any rate) a bit hazy. Soon there came the twang of a samisen; then everyone began clapping in rhythm and singing away happily, at which point one of the guests got up and embarked on an island folk dance. After he got tired (or thirsty), another took his place.

In the midst of all this, one of the guests came over to me and, with a happy smile on his face, shook my hand and told me I was a true *sakejō*. This I understood to mean a man who likes his liquor and I accepted it as the compliment it was no doubt intended to be. Certainly I could hardly, at that point, deny it. After a few more songs and a few more words of praise on my drinking ability, I realized that if I was ever to find my bed that night I would have to leave at once. I was the first to go. The other men, it seemed, were just beginning to settle down to some serious drinking. The women, here as at every other Ryukyuan party I went to, drank no alcohol.

When I somewhat hazily reached the front door, my hostess handed me a box wrapped in the customary gift cloth: it contained, I discovered later, all sorts of delicious foods, including fish cakes and fried chicken and *sushi*.

My landlord invited me to another *iwai* on the occasion of his

OKINAWA

father's seventy-third birthday. Long ago, when the Okinawans took over the Chinese lunar calendar, they accepted also the Chinese concept of twelve-year cycles, including the belief that the thirteenth year of life may be a dangerous one, and every twelfth year thereafter. In Okinawa, however, on a person's sixty-first birthday, a special congratulatory party is held, and it is repeated at the end of every twelve-year cycle so long as the man remains alive.

At this iwai, each guest, of whom there were fifty or more, first approached the low table behind which sat *tanme* ("grandfather"). On the table sat a small basket into which the guest dropped a specially prepared envelope containing some money, after which he congratulated *tanme* and then drank down a small cup of sake that the old man had poured out.

Everyone having eaten some of the food on his tray, and the men having made a good start on the liquor, somebody started playing the samisen and the party was suddenly a good deal less formal than it had been earlier. Then I noticed men beginning to move around the room, bowing to relatives and friends and filling glasses. Oh, oh, I thought, here we go again. But I had learned my lesson: when my glass was filled, I sipped rather than gulped. I knew that I was behaving improperly and, what is even worse, tarnishing my hard-won reputation as a *sakejō* but I hoped the fact that I was a mere gaijin made the whole matter altogether irrelevant.

Another kind of iwai, but one that follows much the same pattern, is the wedding reception. The Japanese-style ceremony itself, usually held in the groom's house or in a shrine such as Naha'a Nami-no-Ue, is frequently (as we shall see) anticlimactic and usually very simple, consisting of little more than the rite known as the *sansan-kudo* ("three-three-nine-times," or forever), in which bride

ISLES OF COURTESY

and groom take three sips three times of sake poured out of special bottles. Once the marriage has been decided upon, however, and the terms mutually agreed to, there is a great deal of planning before the ceremony itself. For one thing, visits must be made to either a shaman or a fortune teller to ensure that the couple's birth years, according to the cycle of twelve, are compatible and then to choose a day that is not antagonistic to either of the participants. In selecting the time for the ceremony, the tide is an all-important factor: it is considered highly desirable that the ceremony be held as the tide starts to rise and that the formal part of the reception be completed before the tide begins to recede.

It is the reception that has become the chief preoccupation, for where once, I was told, this was a relatively simple iwai for the mass of the people, it has grown increasingly elaborate in recent years, and now each couple tries to stage a reception that will outdo all other receptions. Since literally hundreds of friends and relatives are invited, the expense can be a great burden for people of modest income. Part of that expense, but only part, is defrayed by the money envelopes that each guest leaves on a table as he enters.

At the reception to which I was invited, the bride and groom sat at the head table, along with their parents and the go-between, who had arranged the marriage, and his wife. The bride wore a brilliantly colored and decorated kimono and a huge wig with a square headpiece to hide, so they say, the horns of jealousy. Her face was so heavily made up—dead white skin and bright red lips—that I could hardly recognize her. The groom, who was a crane operator at the docks, wore a Westernstyle morning suit, with a long tailcoat and striped trousers. During this formal part of the reception, while the go-between and other selected guests expatiated upon the ster-

OKINAWA ⛩

ling qualities of the young couple, the bride stared fixedly at the table, her face an expressionless mask. Perhaps, poor thing, she had no choice, with all that heavy white pigment and powder. Meantime, the guests had unwrapped the boxes of food in front of them and nibbled away as the speakers droned on, the bride stared down, and the clearly uncomfortable groom sweated profusely.

After the speeches finally ended (and I had begun to fear they never would), the bride and groom left the reception hall to return shortly, the bride looking like herself again, without that extraordinary makeup and head gear and wearing a Western-style evening gown instead of the traditional kimono. The bridal couple resumed their places at the head table, and now the reception suddenly turned informal; perhaps, for the newlyweds, overly so, since the master of ceremonies, who had previously introduced the guest speakers, now began to make broad jokes and to ask embarrassing questions of the bride and groom, all to general hilarity. However, since the bride is frequently several months pregnant by the time the wedding takes place, I decided the questions were not all that embarrassing.

In former days, here as in both Japan and China, an arranged marriage was the customary thing, but of recent years love matches have become increasingly prevalent. In either case, it still seems to be the custom for the groom to give the bride's parents a certain amount of money before the wedding, thus proving his ability to support her. The amount varies of course. In small villages, I was told, it may be the equivalent of about two hundred dollars, in Naha, as much as five hundred dollars. Usually the money goes back to the newly married couple in the form of furniture when the bride moves into her new home.

Another old custom that appears to be on the way out is that

ISLES OF COURTESY

which permitted, or rather encouraged, the young man and woman, once the marriage had been agreed to, to sleep together in the girl's house. They were known, during this period, as the *yung nu miitu* ("the night couple"), and it was hoped that the girl would become pregnant before the wedding ceremony, since childlessness was, and still is in some areas, an acceptable reason for divorce. In any case, both the making and the breaking of a marriage in the Ryukyus seem to a Westerner to be accomplished with enviable ease.

Once the couple is married, they seldom go to parties together, or if they do, they separate on arrival, the wife joining the other women, the husband joining the other men. If the husband's company gives a party, his wife is not invited; and when he introduces her he always speaks of her as his "foolish wife." Although these practices reflect the old-fashioned Japanese way of treating women, they give an altogether untrue picture of female status in Ryukyuan society. And this brings up the complex question of religion in the islands, for here women play a dominant role.

Anthropologists and sociologists, chiefly Japanese and American, have written fat tomes on the subject, so I shall attempt no detailed exegesis here beyond noting that of equal importance with the shamans (*yuta*) are the priestesses (*nuru*), of whom there are many different kinds, with different duties. Of lesser importance in ecclesiastical circles are fortunetellers, sorcerers, Buddhist priests, and healers.

A more generic term for the priestess is *kaminchu*, which gives a clue to her chief function, that is, the propitiation of the *kami* sacred to the particular group for whom she is acting. The Ryukyuan *kami* are similar to the Japanese but far more embracing in that they may be a natural force or phenomenon (such as sky or sea), an im-

OKINAWA

portant everyday object (hearth or well), an occupational symbol (boat or bellows), an illustrious ancestor, or a living person who has been embued with the spirit of the kami. This person is known as a *kaminchu* and may be either male or female, although female *kaminchu* are far more usual. *Nuru,* whether village priestesses, state priestesses, or kami priestesses, are of course always women. Probably one reason the kami play so much more striking a role in Okinawa than in contemporary Japan is that Buddhism never achieved the dominance in the Ryukyus that it did in Japan once it was introduced there from China, by way of Korea, in the sixth century A.D.

An older sister appears to be of more importance in a man's spiritual life than his wife. Men have told me, for example, that when they went off to be soldiers in the imperial Japanese army, they carried with them a lock of their sister's hair and a bit of cloth that she had woven. The belief persisted throughout the islands that it was the sister's spirit that had the power to protect her brother; if, however, he failed to show her the proper respect, she had the equivalent power to lay a curse upon him and bring him to harm.

This close relationship is said to go back to the beginning of time, when a divine brother and sister came down from heaven to earth and formed the Ryukyu Islands. They took up their residence, according to one legend, on the small island of Kudaka, near the southern tip of Okinawa, and there, with the help of a passing wind, the goddess became pregnant and gave birth to five children, three boys and two girls. The eldest son became the first king of the islands, the second son the first lord (*anji*), and the third the first farmer. Thus were initiated the three classes of ancient Okinawan society. Of the two girls, the elder became the first state priestess,

ISLES OF COURTESY

the younger the first community priestess.

I dutifully made the pilgrimage to Kudaka, a flat island two miles long and half a mile wide, and to the small weather-beaten shack on the edge of the village that marks, so I was told, the spot where mankind began his existence. Until 1673, Okinawan kings made a similar pilgrimage; after that they contented themselves with going to the tip of Chinen Peninsula, which overlooks Kudaka. I was disappointed in the cradle of man: no lush vegetation, no tempting fruit—only a few large trees that had contrived to withstand the last typhoon. It was not my idea of the Garden of Eden, although there remains a sacred grove on the island where once every twelve years, during the year of the horse, nuru perform special rites.

When a woman marries, she assumes charge of religious practices in her husband's house, but at the same time she maintains her premarital tie with her father's or elder brother's house. Thus she may have two households to look after, insofar as its kami relationships are concerned, and it devolves upon her to report to the spirits of her husband's ancestors such important occurrences as may concern them. Neither Buddhism nor Confucianism figured largely in ancient, female-dominated Okinawan religious life, although with later Japanese insistence on the importance of both some intermingling of religious practices was inevitable. As in other parts of Japan, Buddhism in the Ryukyus became associated with the afterlife as well as with ancestor worship, which was never of prime importance in older Okinawan religious practices.

Of more significance is the fact that on the first and fifteenth day of every lunar month the female head of a household reports to the *fi nu kang* (*hi no kami* in Japanese), the kami of fire or, in this case, of the hearth, the symbol and focus of the household. In older days,

OKINAWA 🛕

every house had a three-stone hearth, where the semimonthly rite was carried out; nowadays, modern stoves have supplanted the hearth, but somewhere in most Ryukyuan kitchens, however modern, there will be an imitation hearth, perhaps only a bowl full of ashes with three stones, to which will come the woman of the house to ensure that the kami is content.

Time and again, I received the impression that Ryukyuan religion had little or nothing to do with ethical or moral principles as we conceive them in the West but rather was chiefly concerned with the correct performance of ritual. When trouble strikes, a Ryukyuan is likely to decide that something has gone wrong with the ritual, and instead of family members trying to solve the problem themselves, the eldest female will take herself off to consult a shaman. Like the priestess, the shaman is almost invariably a woman; people tend, in fact, to suspect the masculinity of a male shaman.

The shaman, or *yuta,* is, like the nuru, a kaminchu: that is to say, she possesses supernatural powers that enable her to communicate with a kami; and for the equivalent of two dollars she will do so and pass the information on to the troubled family. Most young people say they have no confidence in the yuta; others suggest that although she possesses no supernatural power, the yuta serves a useful purpose in alleviating anxiety. Whenever I asked them if they consult a yuta, they would almost always reply no, adding however that their mothers or grandmothers did, particularly if someone in the family was ill.

Once, in Yakena, I watched a yuta treating a sick baby. After talking with the mother for a while, she placed her hand on the baby's brow, closed her eyes, prayed silently, and then blew gently two or three times. Having repeating this process several times, she

ISLES OF COURTESY

assured the mother that the baby would be all right, after which the mother paid the fee and went away comforted. I was impressed by the authoritative bearing of the yuta, and I could understand how it might well have a calming effect, but I rather doubted that the yuta could effectively take the place of a good doctor if anything were seriously wrong. It is the sort of thing that, in more "enlightened" countries, is called faith healing, and works equally well.

Another source of help during illness is that offered by *yabuu*, which means moxa but also refers to two widely divergent types of practitioner. Both appear to share a common belief that the origin of the illness is supernatural, arising from the antagonism of a kami. In other ways, however, the two types of *yabuu* differ. One has studied either Chinese or Japanese medicine, and must pass an examination before being granted a license to practice by the government. The other, although he may have a wide folk knowledge of medicinal plants, tends to rely on ancient ritual to exorcise the illness. It is this latter who more properly fulfills the dictionary definition of the Japanese word *yabuisha*, "a quack doctor." The former, however well trained he may be, is fast disappearing from Ryukyuan life as the number of its accredited M.D.'s increases.

Extremely complex are the various rites attending death in the islands, and of them all perhaps the most characteristically Ryukyuan is the bone-washing ceremony. Unlike other Japanese, the islanders did not, until recently, adopt cremation as the most efficient way to deal with a dead body. Accordingly, some still bury their dead with great ceremony in a turtle-backed or omega-shaped tomb; after the second or third year, they remove the remains, clean away whatever may still be clinging to the bones, wash them in distilled rice spirits, and place them in a burial urn. After thirty-three years, the bones are taken from the urn and deposited on a high platform to join the bones of other ancestors. Here there are various levels, each representing a different stage of advancement into the spirit world. The bodies of kaminchu bypass the bone-washing stage, for they are already pure, inasmuch as they partake of divinity.

Every human being is the possessor of a life spirit called the *mabui*: while he lives, the spirit is known as the *ichi mabui*; after death, as the *shini mabui*. Collectively, the spirits of the dead, especially male and female ancestors in a direct line, are known as *futuki*, a word that has connections with the Buddhist term *hotoke* (in colloquial Japanese, the deceased or the soul of the deceased). Following the Satsuma invasion in the seventeenth century, Buddhism was imposed more and more stringently on indigenous Okinawan religious practices, with the result that households began building Budddist altars, called *buchidang* (*butsudan* in Japanese, after Butsu, the Buddha), which eventually acquired, and still maintain, a sanctity second only to that of the hearth. Japanese ancestral worship, however, was never adopted in its total form: it was merely grafted on to the native religion, which continued to insist on the importance of pure ritual. Nowadays, Okinawans respect the *futuki* and report regularly to them, as other Japanese do; but, unlike the others, they do so not out of piety but rather in the hope of remaining on good terms with the *futuki* and preventing their taking any disagreeable action against the living. As one Okinawan friend explained to me, "When we celebrate a festival, it is never for ourselves alone. Our ancestors too enjoy the festivities, and we are always very careful to offer food and drink at the *buchidang*. It is very important that we should never offend our ancestors. We must always keep them in mind when observing our festivals."

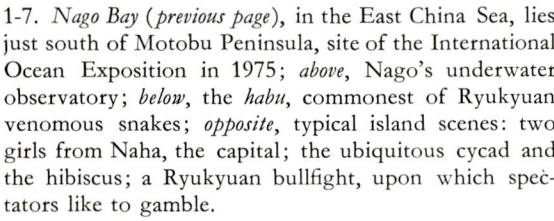

1-7. *Nago Bay* (*previous page*), in the East China Sea, lies just south of Motobu Peninsula, site of the International Ocean Exposition in 1975; *above*, Nago's underwater observatory; *below*, the *habu*, commonest of Ryukyuan venomous snakes; *opposite*, typical island scenes: two girls from Naha, the capital; the ubiquitous cycad and the hibiscus; a Ryukyuan bullfight, upon which spectators like to gamble.

8-10. *Rice* is a slowly vanishing crop in the Ryukyus because of the scarcity of suitable land and the gruelling work, which brings in poor returns. *Below*, rice straw is dried in the field and a woman sets out rice seedlings; *right*, small paddies near Nago.

11-13. *Pineapples* now occupy about eight percent of all Ryukyuan arable land. *Below*, fruit growing in the once arid northern hills of Okinawa: *opposite*, the blossoming flower and freshly picked fruit ready to be taken to the local cannery.

14-15. *Two sights* that are favorites with the Okinawans are this torii (*above*) overlooking the churning East China Sea and the coral caves (*left*) along west coast beaches.

16-19. *Water, water everywhere!* *Above left,* a resident of Nago's underwater observatory; *above right,* a small crag jutting out into the sea; *left,* multicolored coral of the Ryukyuan underwater world and "star sand," actually fossil shells of Foraminifera.

20. Ōshima (*overleaf*), a small ▶ island off Okinawa's southeast coast, is now joined to the main island by an arched, typhoon-resistant bridge.

21-25. *Sugar cane*, the Ryukyus' chief crop, supplies over thirty percent of total farm income and more than forty percent of all exports. *Above left*, silver flowers glistening in the winter sun mean that the cane will soon be ready for harvesting; *below left*, the cane is carried to the nearest road, where it is left to be picked up by trucks. *Right*, cane passes through four evaporators that reduce it to syrup; *below*, a mountain of dried sugar waits for shipment to Kyushu or Honshu, where it will be refined.

27. *Tattooing*, seen now only on the hands of old women, is said to have been begun in the sixteenth century to help prevent pirates from carrying off Ryukyuan girls to be sold as prostitutes.

26. *Mortar and pestle* of ancient origin are still used to crush grain on the island of Taketomi in the Yaeyama group.

28. *A bride* at an Okinawan marriage ceremony wears traditional Japanese wedding kimono.

29. *The yuta*, priestesses of the native religion, practice fortune telling and faith healing, both declining in popularity among the younger generation.

30. *Rice cakes*, wrapped in fragrant leaves, provide a treat for children as well as a protection against illness during Muuchii, "the driving-out-devils festival," held in the twelfth lunar month.

31. *The household ancestral shrine* is loaded with gifts and special foods during Bon, the midsummer festival when the souls of the ancestors are welcomed home for a happy visit.

32. *A three-stone hearth* (*below left*) in a tiny hut on the island of Kudaka, off Okinawa's southeast coast, is said to mark the birthplace of man.

33. *Family tombs* in a turtle-back shape (*below*), a conspicuous feature of the Okinawan landscape, may house the bones of literally hundreds of ancestors.

34. *Offerings* at this tomb indicate that a death has occurred within the past forty-nine days. In addition to sandals, other useful items such as an umbrella and a cane, as well as food, may be left for the use of the departed.

35. *Paper fortunes* are hung during New Year's festivities on a sacred cherry tree in front of Futenma's Shinto shrine.

38. *Ishigaki* (*overleaf*), another ▶
of the smaller islands, has tree-
covered mountains in the north
and in the south wide green
plains where animals pasture
peacefully.

36-37. *A natural arch* carved by
the waves pierces this *sunayama*
("sand hill") on the northwest-
ern coast of Miyako Island.
Hirara (*below*), also on Miyako,
is famous for its well-stocked
shops and immaculately clean
streets. A flat island, Miyako is
rich in sugar cane—and clever
businessmen.

39-40. *Island flora*: amid the lush forests of Ishigaki rise the coconut palm, the banyan tree and the mangrove. The grotesque "looking-glass tree" (*sakishima suonoki*) is fast disappearing from the islands because of its usefulness in boat construction.

42. *Thatched roofs* are customarily reinforced with vines as a protection against typhoons on Ishigaki Island.

41. *Waterfalls* appear unexpectedly in Ishigaki's richly verdant forests.

43. *Tatami ishi* ("mat stones," overleaf), on a small island near Kumejima, were once thought to have been laid down by the gods in a prankish mood. Actually, the "mats" were formed by molten lava as it cooled; a beer bottle indicates their size.

Isles of Festivity

The observance of Ryukyuan festivals is a most stimulating subject, but also one that involves the unbelievably complex question of the Ryukyuan calendar, based originally on the corrected Chinese lunar calendar. So, too, at one time, was that of Japan, but after Japan's adoption of the Gregorian, lunar dates, especially when they marked important holidays, were simply assigned a place in the solar calendar. For example, the third day of the third lunar month was anciently given over to a holiday for young girls, the fifth day of the fifth lunar month to one for boys; after the adoption of the solar calendar, the two holidays, which would wander up and down the solar year, were permanently fixed on March 3 and May 5. With the Japanese administration of Okinawa came the introduction of the Gregorian calendar, but Okinawans have persistently resisted this particular reformation, at least insofar as their agricultural cycle, their essential fortune telling, and their observance of traditional festivals are concerned. One happy result, at least for working Okinawans, is that some holidays are celebrated twice, once by solar and once by lunar reckoning.

To me it is astonishing that the Chinese, lacking electronic computers as they did several thousand years ago, were able to

OKINAWA 🏯

evolve their twelve-month lunar calendar, inserting seven intercalary months into every nineteen-year period in order to make lunar time agree with solar time. This was only the beginning of Chinese calendar lore, but as far as I am concerned (lacking a built-in abacus), it is also the end. I am quite unable to fathom all the complexities, ramifications, and vagaries of the labyrinthine Chinese time system, but I can easily understand why the masters of the Middle Kingdom exacted rich tribute in return for passing on their comprehensive almanacs, which told farmers when to sow and when to reap and which proved invaluable aids to fortune tellers and other diviners of the future.

Festivals take a fair share of Ryukyuan time and energy, and a sign of the times is that among city people some now pass unobserved. Younger people who have left their villages to live and work in the large towns seem disappointed by the dullness that results from this lack of interest. In the country, however, festivals are still celebrated with all their ancient verve, and I suspect the day when Okinawans will willingly relinquish entirely their immemorial festivities is a long, long way off.

New Year's festivities on the main islands follow a traditional pattern and preparations begin, some days before New Year's Eve, with the paying of old debts, refurbishing the house, buying some new clothes, and making the traditional cakes of pounded rice called *mochi*. The solar New Year's Eve itself is a festive family time (not, as in the West, an excuse for large parties), and on New Year's Day many people go to a temple or a shrine or else do their praying at the family altar.

The Okinawan lunar New Year is something else again. It lasts for three days and features a great deal of jollity, including lengthy

ISLES OF FESTIVITY

all male drinking parties, the killing and roasting of a pig, and all sorts of games for children. In very remote areas the custom still survives of drawing fresh water from a well or spring on the first morning, and in the city of boiling tap water, water which every member of the family uses for his first ablutions of the year. Then the leading male decorates the house with pine and bamboo and hangs a special straw decoration over the door.

It is a time of communal visiting, and it is important that the first to set off are young boys, who are said to bring good luck to the households they visit. In return they are given a small gift of money (perhaps about twenty-five cents), but obviously if they visit enough houses they can amass a good-sized fortune before the girls start scurrying around on their tour of visits. Days before, children begin counting up how much money they are likely to receive, and on the eve of the festivities they are so excited they hardly sleep at all.

Then comes the time for adult visiting: women chat and pray and men drink. Some have told me that they recall, as children, seeing men so drunk after a round of visits that they were quite unable to walk. Along with the eating and the drinking and the gossiping, there is the buying of a fortune-telling paper at a shrine, which, after the paper is read, is either kept or tied to a sacred tree nearby. The village nuru holds special rites during the three-day period, and many families engage the services of a yuta.

Other first-month festivities are devoted to commemorating family members who have died during the previous year and then, a few days later, on the twentieth, glorifying the girls of Tsuji. Set aside as a licensed quarter back in the seventeenth century, Tsuji was destroyed by bombs in 1944 and rebuilt shortly thereafter without a marked change of character. The festival is an ancient one, its origins lost in myth, but all the variations seem to agree on at least one point: a girl of high rank was abducted and found herself working in the Tsuji quarter. Since her family was too lofty to hold any communication with the girl, even their own daughter, who hired herself out for purposes of entertainment, she evolved a scheme whereby she and her family could at least have a glimpse of each other during that all-important first month. She persuaded the other girls who worked in the teahouses of Tsuji to join her in the quarter's business promotion procession, and so she was able to see her family, who sat in a reviewing stand along the route of the parade, and they were able to see her without a loss of face on either side.

In fact, she went so far, the legend goes, as to sing a song of greeting for her family as she passed, a song that the family returned. This led to the girls of Tsuji achieving a place in the society of the capital that had previously been denied them, and the parade of the teahouse girls still continues. The parade begins at the Under the Pine teahouse, which is more famous under another name—Teahouse of the August Moon.

On the third day of the third lunar month comes the Girls' Festival. On this day women and girls go to the beaches for a picnic lunch and after low tide enter the rising water. This custom, too, is an ancient one, and it also concerns a girl of good family who got in trouble. Having received the amorous attentions of an unscrupulous *akamataa* (a snake spirit with the power to become a handsome prince), she soon found herself pregnant. In despair, she confided in one of her ladies-in-waiting, who advised her to wash herself in the sea. The ablution worked miraculously well, and today Ryukyuan

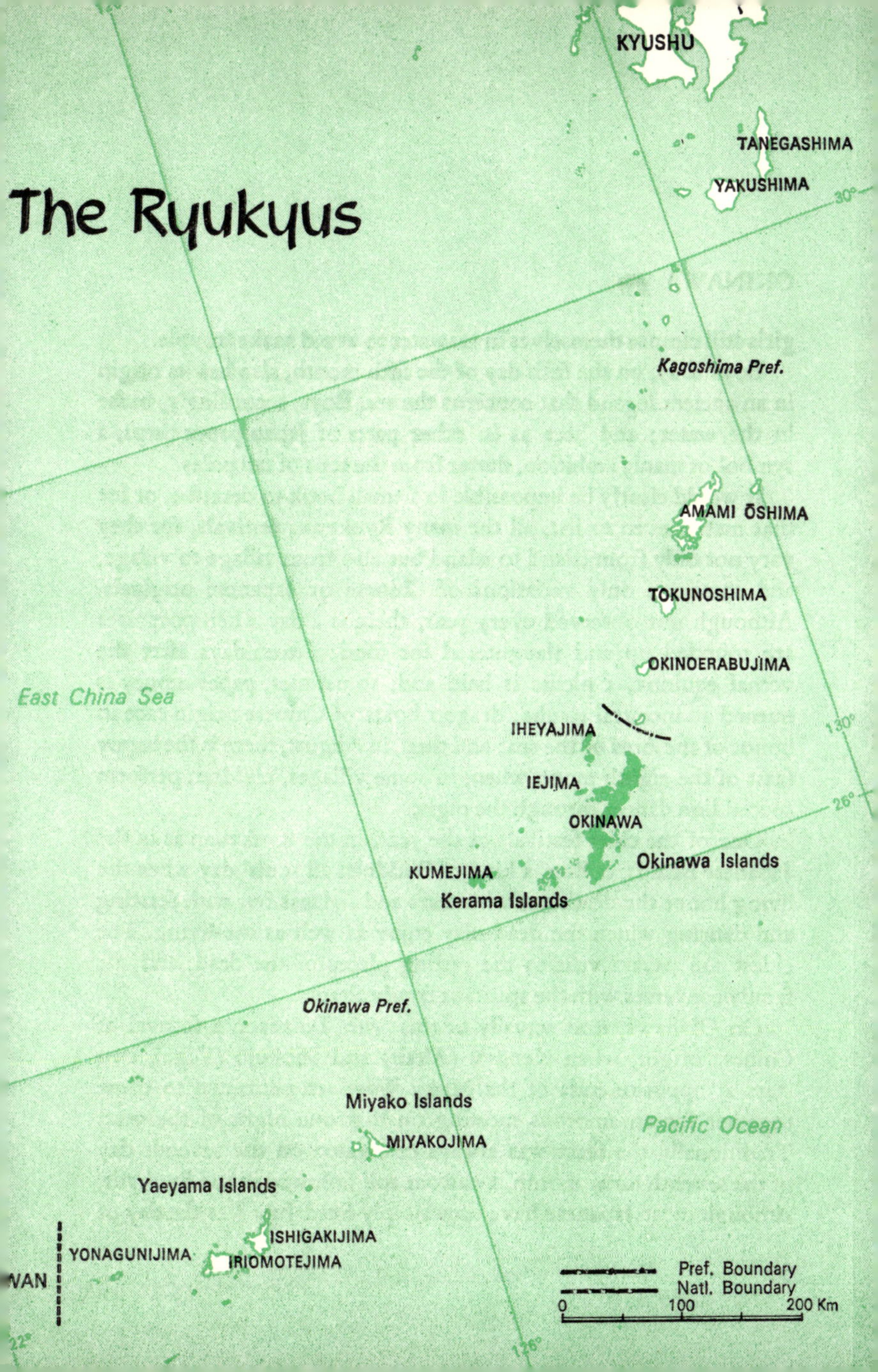

The Ryukyus

KYUSHU

TANEGASHIMA
YAKUSHIMA

Kagoshima Pref.

AMAMI ŌSHIMA

TOKUNOSHIMA

OKINOERABUJIMA

East China Sea

IHEYAJIMA

IEJIMA

OKINAWA

KUMEJIMA   Okinawa Islands
Kerama Islands

Okinawa Pref.

Miyako Islands
MIYAKOJIMA

Pacific Ocean

Yaeyama Islands

YONAGUNIJIMA   ISHIGAKIJIMA
               IRIOMOTEJIMA

Pref. Boundary
Natl. Boundary
0   100   200 Km

OKINAWA

girls still cleanse themselves in seawater to avoid snake trouble.

Boys' Day, on the fifth day of the fifth month, also has its origin in an ancient legend that concerns the sea. Boys, accordingly, bathe in the water; and here as in other parts of Japan paper carps, a symbol of manly ambition, flutter from the tops of tall poles.

It would clearly be impossible in a small book to describe, or for that matter even to list, all the many Ryukyuan festivals, for they vary not only from island to island but also from village to village, and some are only variations of Chinese or Japanese originals. Although not observed every year, there is a day when porpoises are rounded up and slaughtered for food; fifteen days after the vernal equinox, a picnic is held and, sometimes, paper money is burned at ancestral tombs; dragon boats of Chinese origin race in honor of the *kami* of the sea; and then, in August, there is the happy feast of the eighth moon when, in some villages, children perform special lion dances through the night.

One of the chief festivals of the year, in the Ryukyuan as in the Japanese islands, is Bon, a kind of Buddhist all souls' day when the living honor the dead, not with tears and sadness but with feasting and dancing which the dead may enjoy as well as the living. The eldest son pays a visit to the resting places of the dead, and the family converses with the spirits at family altars.

On Okinawa, Bon actually begins with Tanabata, a festival of Chinese origin, when Kengyū (Altair) and Shokujo (Vega), two stars at opposite ends of the Milky Way, are permitted to come together for an amorous meeting on that one night of the year. Traditionally the feast was always celebrated on the seventh day of the seventh lunar month, a custom still followed in the Ryukyus, although most Japanese have now simply fixed July 7 as the day of

ISLES OF FESTIVITY

the Star Festival. On Okinawa, however, coming as it does exactly six days before the beginning of Bon, Tanabata is thought of as a kind of preparatory holiday. "On that day," one Okinawan told me, "we cut the grass around our tombs and put them in order. Then we say to our ancestors: 'In six days we will be expecting you, and we will have delicious food prepared for you'."

Bon itself lasts for three days, from the thirteenth through the fifteenth of the seventh lunar month. Its purposes are not only to invite and entertain the spirits of the dead but also to ensure that they depart on time, in an orderly and harmless fashion.

One of the girl students in my English class wrote an essay in which she said that on the night of the thirteenth her father, after setting torches out on either side of the gate of their house, invited the ancestors to come to the buchidang, where special dishes had been meticulously laid out. In addition to cooked food and fruit, there were stalks of sugarcane to serve as walking sticks for the spirits.

Every member of the family comes home for Bon, if he possibly can, no matter how far away he may be, to pay his respects to the dead and to enjoy the feasting and the happy conversation that accompany the reunion. During the two days that follow, family members from time to time wander over to the buchidang, bow their heads, clasp their hands, and address a few words to the ancestors, who must never be allowed to feel that they have been forgotten or neglected. On the second day the living exchange gifts and give presents to the dead. Then, on the last night, lanterns or torches are lit again, and the spirits are courteously invited to leave the buchidang and return to the tomb. Baskets, filled by the women with food and other gifts, have been prepared for the de-

OKINAWA

parting dead, and all the living accompany the spirits to the gate, chattering happily with them. After burning a few strips of paper money, family members bid the spirits farewell until their next visit the following year.

On Okinawa, once the spirits have begun their journey back to the tomb, the living congregate at an appointed place in the village or town to take part in a special dance (*eisa*), which may start as early as eight in the evening and continue until four the following morning. Since Bon ends on the fifteenth day of the lunar month, there is always a full moon; in some villages paper lanterns are hung in the dance area to provide more light and visual pleasure. Girls customarily wear light summer kimonos, and boys don colorful uniforms that represent their village. Indeed, the beating of the drums and the plunk of the samisen, the dancing and the singing, the hand-clapping and loud happy whistling all combine to make for an unforgettable night. Not all of the Ryukyuan Islands, incidentally, have a Bon Odori on the last night, as this community dance is called in Japanese: on Yaeyama, for example, the Bon Odori is replaced by the performance of a drama and a dance by a single chosen couple.

Among all the Ryukyuan festivals I attended, I found one of the most fascinating to be that which takes place in the north of Okinawa, along Shioya bay, on the first "day of the pig" following the end of Bon. On the eve of the festivities, priestesses (*nuru*) of the village of Taminato go to the *kami ashagi*, a walless shelter used by the priestesses for public rites. There, having cleansed themselves, they spend the entire night chanting ancient Ryukyuan poems.

Late that same morning, dressed now in kimonos woven out of banana fibers, the naru return to the *kami ashagi*, where they pray

ISLES OF FESTIVITY

andthen partake of a special drink made of sake and rice gruel, which is said to possess healing and protective powers. Then, accompanied by people from Taminato, they walk to Yako, a nearby village that boasts a more imposing *kami ashagi* than that of Taminato. There, having taken part in additional rites and special dances, the priestesses change their banana-cloth kinomos for white ones. Toward two in the afternoon, the general population begins to move down to the water for the forthcoming boat race; at the same time three priestesses go to the end of the bay, where three large boats are waiting, each manned by about forty oarsmen and each representing one of the three villages on the bay. After the three priestesses have taken their places in separate boats, the race begins.

As it continues, watched from the shore by thousands of visitors, the chief nuru and other priestesses of rank ride in palanquins through the village of Shioya down to the sea, where they perform rites intended to ensure good fishing for all the villagers. After the boat race ends, wrestlers take part in sumo matches (Okinawan style) under the eyes of the priestesses, who by this time have completed their ritual duties.

All over Okinawa, as well as on the other islands, there are so many exciting sights to see, things to do, objects to buy that an energetic visitor would be busy every day of the year. I shall have to content myself with mentioning only a few of the things that have most impressed me.

Okinawa itself, as the largest and most populous of the Ryukyus, offers, naturally enough, the greatest attractions for the visitor. Naha, under the Japanese, became the Ryukyuan administrative capital in 1879, and the chief sights of interest are to be found in the Shuri quarter of the city, for Shuri was the political, religious,

OKINAWA

and cultural capital for over a thousand years.

Unhappily, the battle for Okinawa was not only, to use Sato's phrase, the bloodiest of the war but was also one of the most culturally and artistically destructive. The great sights of Shuri, including the greatest of all, the old royal castle, were all bombed to smithereens, and many treasures simply vanished. However, the Okinawa Prefecture museum, formerly Shuri Museum, contains around four thousand exhibits, including fine old textiles, coronation jewelry, inlaid lacquerware, two of the capital's ancient bronze bells, and a model of the castle's audience hall. On the site of the castle itself there now stands the University of the Ryukyus, opened in 1950; three years later, the broadcasting station of the Ryukyus was also installed here; and in 1958 there began the reconstruction, on the original site, of the Shurei no Mon. Despite all the postwar building, however, there are still stone vestiges of the original castle to be seen.

Back in the fifteenth century, on a ridge five hundred feet above Nakagusuku Bay, Nakagusuku Castle was erected to help protect Shuri against invasions from the north. During the last war, the bay was used as a major military harbor; now, where great warships once sought anchorage, oil tankers and a few small and innocuous fishing vessels ply their peaceful trade. Less than a quarter of a mile away stands a country house built in the eighteenth century by a prosperous farmer. Erected entirely without the use of iron, it suggests what houses within Nakagusuku Castle must have been like.

Nami-no-ue Shrine, the most famous in the Ryukyus, and the Buddhist temple called Gokokuji were both wholly destroyed during the war and both have been rebuilt. Nami-no-ue is once again

ISLES OF FESTIVITY

a popular shrine for wedding ceremonies, and from a spot not far away begins the annual procession of girls known variously as tea-house dancers, geishas, or prostitutes, depending on how the speaker feels on the subject.

There are, of course, a number of tragic mementos of the war in Okinawa such as the command post burrowed in a hill a mile and a half east of Naha, where Vice Admiral Minoru Ōta and his staff, seeing that defeat was inevitable, committed suicide; Kuniyoshi ridge, where Lieutenant General Simon Bolivar Buckner, overall commander of the Allied forces in the battle for Okinawa, was killed; and, not far away, "Suicide Hill," so-called, where the Japanese commander, Lieutenant General Mitsuru Ushijima, took his own life, calling on his troops to continue the battle. Anyone who would visit the chief sites of the battle for Okinawa should first go to the Armed Forces Museum at Fort Buckner, which has a three-dimensional map of the island and an accompanying recorded history of the battle.

More peacefully inclined visitors will want to see what Ryukyuan arts are like, performing arts as well as the islands' many thriving folk crafts. The latter may be observed in progress (and of course patronized) almost everywhere, but the only theater in all the Ryukyus that features regular performances of drama, dance, and music is Naha's Okiei; Shimpo hall, also in Naha, and the Naha Gekijo have special occasional performances; and native-style dances are often the chief form of entertainment in cabarets featuring Ryukyuan food. Also, of course, there is hardly an island festival that fails to include some folk dancing and singing, and even when only a couple of families get together someone is sure to bring out the Okinawan version of the samisen, which soon results in a gay evening of

ISLES OF FESTIVITY

singing and dancing.

This familiar stringed instrument apparently reached Japan from China by way of the Ryukyus, where it was known originally as a *jyamisen*. The word is still used to differentiate the Okinawan instrument, whose sound box is covered with snakeskin, from the Japanese instrument, although Okinawans commonly refer to it by the modern Japanese name. Other Ryukyuan musical instruments, played either solo or in groups, are bamboo flutes, drums, and a thirteen-stringed harp which resembles but is not identical with the Japanese *koto*.

Drama, dance and music in Okinawa all demonstrate the profound effect that not only China and Japan but also Southeast Asia have exercised in ages past upon the culture of the island kingdom. Ryukyuans use the five-tone scale rather than the octave; they dispense with the harmony that is so familiar to Western ears; and singers' voices are generally nasal and pitched high, some using a kind of throaty twang that sound almost as if they had swallowed a Jews' harp. Dances, here as elsewhere in the Far East, are usually based on stylized patterns of gesture and posture that are familiar and therefore meaningful to the audience, although there does exist one dance of free expression, known as the *kachashi*. *Kumidori*, musical dramas written originally in the eighteenth century for the entertainment of visiting Chinese dignitaries, also feature native Ryukyuan dance forms.

Without stirring very far from the center of Naha, the visitor may see most of the Ryukyus' justly admired folk crafts in action. Tsuboya, for instance, where many Okinawan potters have their wheels and their kilns, was once a separate village but is now part of the growing capital city. Looking rather like a dilapidated slum

OKINAWA

area, Tsuboya has very narrow streets and tired old houses; most of its potteries are hidden away behind high fences, as though the potters were indifferent to Okinawa's increasing tourist trade. Indeed, many of their products exhibit a simplicity and a serenity that seem far removed from our bustling and harassed postwar world. Some of Tsuboya's potters, to be sure, have small kilns on the spot and modern showrooms, but most still use ancient low-temperature kilns built into the side of the hill nearby, and some still turn the wheel as their ancestors did long ago—by kicking it with their feet.

Perhaps of all handcrafts, the most typically Ryukyuan are their textiles, of which there is a wide variety based on different methods of cloth making, weaving, and dyeing. *Kasuri*, for instance, is the name given to the most frequently encountered kind of weaving, where the design is indicated on the loom by the placing of predyed spotted threads. Still another type of weaving is *hanaori*, which uses a raised pattern in many colors on both warp and woof. *Bingata* features a method of dyeing not altogether unlike that of Javanese batiks, although here the wax of the Javanese process is replaced by a resist made of rice bran, rice flour and salt; the result is the most brilliantly colored of all Okinawan textiles.

These crafts may be observed in or very near Naha, but if the visitor would watch the ancient and intricate technique of producing banana cloth (*bashōfu*), he must journey to the village of Kijoka, near Okuma, in northern Okinawa. The entire process from the stripping of the banana plant, through the elaborate processing of the fibers, to the spinning, dyeing, and weaving of the cloth is performed by women of the village. Once upon a time this difficult and time-consuming technique was practiced all over Okinawa;

ISLES OF FESTIVITY

soon it will probably have disappeared entirely, and Ryukyuan banana-plant textiles will be visible only in museums.

Lacquerware and glassware, both highly prized Ryukyuan exports, could hardly be more dissimilar in origin. Most lacquerware is made from the *deigo*, a short tree with light gray bark that produces a scarlet torch-shaped flower in the spring. At any of Naha's three chief producers, the visitor may watch the ancient and complex process of turning the wood into a bowl or a tray, of sanding it smooth, and then of lacquering it and perhaps inlaying bits of mother-of-pearl. Okinawan glassware, on the other hand, received its main impetus only after the war, when discarded bottles of various sorts were melted down by thrifty Okinawan glassmakers in a very hot oven, given a handsome new shape, and then placed in another oven to cool slowly. Especially popular now are fish-shaped flower vases, bunches of grapes, glass flowers and decorative bottles.

Anyone who is interested in Ryukyuan handcraft must not, certainly, limit himself to Okinawa, for many of the smaller islands still practice their ancient arts, chiefly weaving. On Kumejima, which, incidentally, is a paradise for fishermen, women make a special kind of pongee (*tsumugi*) out of silk, using dyes produced locally from island plants and soil. One *tan*, which is some eleven yards long by fourteen inches wide, takes a woman more than a month to produce and sold, when I was there, for the equivalent of about $150.

Then there is the island of Miyako, whose women have long been famous for their weaving of fine-quality linen, a dark ramie cloth with white kasuri designs. Coral is also one of Miyako's exports, and one of its imports is tourists, who come to enjoy the

OKINAWA

island's new hotels and its splendid golf courses. It is a flat island, and as such it must protect itself against the threat of typhoons by building strong concrete houses. Miyako grows a great deal of sugarcane, a hardy crop likely to survive almost everything but a direct hit by a savage typhoon.

Ishigaki, slightly larger and more mountainous than Miyako, is said to grow the best pineapples in the Ryukyus and is also a producer of livestock. It has been devastated in the past by a great tidal wave (of the kind called tsunami) and by frequent epidemics of malaria that were not brought under control until the American occupation. The women of Ishigaki, like those of Miyako, weave ramie fiber, but here the cloth is usually white with black or brown kasuri designs. Ishigaki is also famous for its lustrous black pearls.

44. *The immemorial New Year's custom* of tying paper fortunes to cherry trees in shrine grounds: after the first day or two, it is hard to find a vacant spot on the tree.

45-46. *Tsuji*, the oldest of Naha's three chief amusement centers, sends out a parade of its teahouse girls on the twentieth day of the first lunar month in honor of the founder of the quarter. Hotei, the patron deity (shown above), one of the seven gods of good fortune, is said to ensure happiness for the girls as well as generosity from their customers.

47-48. *The cherry blossom festival* of Nago, at the end of January or beginning of February, is a popular time for Okinawans to climb Nago Castle Hill between rows of flowering trees.

53. *Annual dance* (overleaf) close the ▶ three-day midsummer Bon festival; each village designs its own distinctive costume.

49-52. *The dragon boat race* at the old Okinawan port of Itoman is of ancient Chinese origin. Three neighboring villages compete, each with a team of twelve oarsmen, a helmsman, and a boy to beat the tempo. Wives of the rowers (*far left*) sing folk songs to cheer their menfolk on, while spectators (*below*), carrying umbrellas against the sun, line the shore. Vessels, decorated for the occasion, are ordinary fishing boats the rest of the year.

54. *Three girls* pause for a rest during the dance; many wear kimonos made from fabric with a splashed pattern (*kasuri*).

55. *Amateur sumo matches*, Ryukyuan style (*below left*), are an integral part of many island festivals.

56. *A Bon dance* (*below*) may begin with the tipsy parading of a jug supposedly filled with distilled rice wine.

57. *The jabisen*, which accompanies almost all Ryukyuan singing and dancing, uses a snakeskin soundboard; the similar three-stringed Japanese samisen uses catskin.

58. *Striped leggings* are a distinctive feature of all men's costumes worn in the village Bon dances.

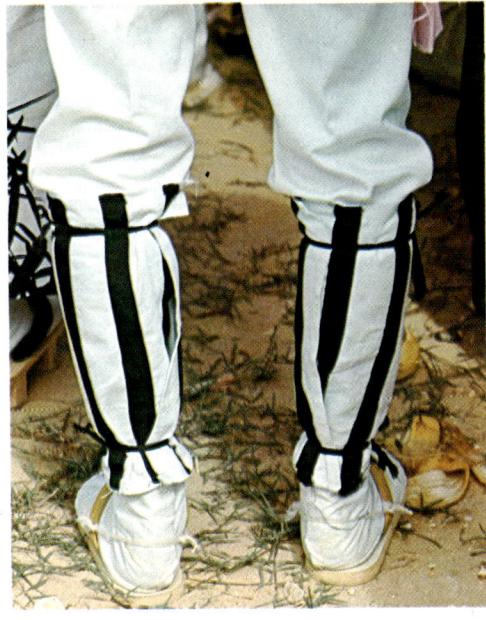

59-60. *Boat races* are held at Shioya Bay in northern Okinawa after the end of the Bon festival. Here as many as forty men from competing villages may man the racing boats, while community priestesses (*left*) gather for the religious rites.

61-62. *Cheering womenfolk* are sometimes so carried away by the excitement of the race that they wade out into the water to encourage the oarsmen. Old-fashioned palanquins are used to carry the priestesses from one Shioya village to another.

63-64. *Rice-straw ropes* at Yonabaru are about three feet in diameter and may be one hundred and fifty yards long. *Below*, male and female ropes (suggesting origins in a fertility rite) are about to be locked together by a pole. As they are brought to the field, young boys (*opposite*) stand on the ropes as symbols of legendary Okinawan warriors.

65-66. *Ryukyuan dance dramas* are a blend of distinctive features from China, Japan and Southeast Asia: *above*, a long and poignant farewell scene; *below*, *Hana no dai* tells the story of how the licensed quarter at Tsuji began, along with the famous parade of the teahouse girls.

67-68. *Musical accompaniment* is supplied by the familiar *jabisen*, drums both large and small (*above*), and the koto (*below*). After each beat, drummers snap their hands upward. The Ryukyuan koto is slightly different from that used in other parts of Japan.

69-73. *Bingata* is the name given to a process of dyeing textiles by means of stencils. Shown above are three examples of modern designs using this technique, while below may be seen the stencil from which the design is taken and the brush used to rub in the dye.

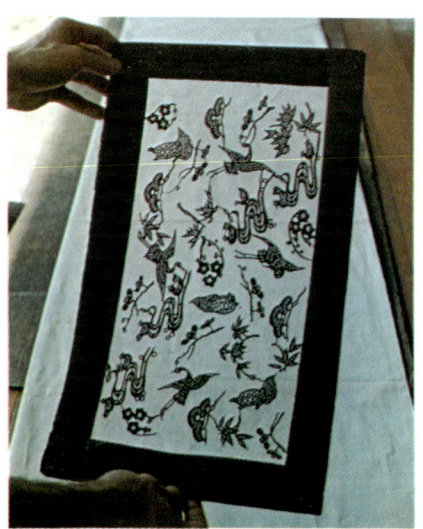 

74-75. *The process* requires a kind of thick paste resist to be applied after the stencil is positioned on the cloth; then the stencil is lifted and moved to the next premarked interval and again covered with paste. The cloth is then laid out in the sun (*right*) for the paste to dry, after which the dye is applied and fixed with soy bean juice. Once the paste has been washed away, the completed fabric is again put out to dry (*below*).

76-79. *The tie-dye technique* is used to produce *kasuri* patterns: *left*, a young woman adjusts her loom while weaving cloth using indigo-dyed threads; *above*, a bundle of freshly dyed threads with strings removed; *below*, two examples of the finished product.

80-82. *Pongee* dyed a distinctive orange brown is produced at Aza-Maja on the island of Kumejima. A dyer (*right*) soaks the threads in a liquid made by boiling chips of reddish wood from local trees (*below right*), then hangs them out to dry (*below left*). Finally they are handwoven by village women on old-fashioned looms.

83. *A Chinese lion* (*above*) from the royal tombs in Shuri was damaged during the Battle of Okinawa in 1945.

84-85. *The pottery center* of modern Okinawa is in the Tsuboya quarter of Naha. *Above,* a potter fashions the familiar Korean dog; *below,* a hillside kiln is ready to be sealed and fired.

86. *A Tsuboya potter* carries on a family tradition stretching back four generations.

87. *A ceramic bottle* has both an incised design and an overglaze known as *akae*, which originated in China.

88. *Red-tiled roofs* are to be seen everywhere in the Ryukyuan islands.

89-91. *Okinawan glassware,* made out of discarded bottles, comes in a bewildering variety of shapes and colors. The glass is melted down and refashioned (at a temperature near 1000° C.), and new colors are achieved by adding various chemicals. Bunches of grapes (*below left*) are especially popular with American shoppers.

Isles of Diplomacy

So far I have said little about the history of the Ryukyus, yet no one can hope to understand them and their people, their sometimes turbulent present and their hopeful future, without knowing a bit about their past. When, in the late nineteenth century, the Japanese took over the Ryukyuan educational system, they preferred to teach children the history of Japan rather than that of their own islands. The reason was obvious enough: Japan, at Western insistence, was just emerging from its thick shell of ancient isolationism. Determined to catch up with the great powers of the West, so as to hold its own against them, it began the building of an empire, an empire of which Liu Ch'iu was to be one of the cornerstones. The aim was to turn the people of Liu Ch'iu, the Ryukyuans, into loyal subjects, and one way of doing that was to shift their allegiance from Shuri to Tokyo, their language from that spoken at home to that spoken on the streets of the Japanese capital, and their knowledge of history from their own to that inaugurated by the Sun Goddess when she sent her grandson down to earth. As a result of this program, together with the disastrous war, and the confusion that followed, few Ryukyuans have even a vague general knowledge of the dramatic story of their islands. Not until 1951 was Ryukyuan history

OKINAWA

added to school curricula. Perhaps it is hardly surprising, then, that the subject should be such an unfamiliar one to foreigners, since it is no less so to Ryukyuans themselves.

This is all the more surprising when one considers what a strategic role the islanders have played in Far Eastern culture. That role was not, it must be noted, of their own choosing. From earliest times on, while they concentrated on earning their daily bread, the world came to them and insisted on being admitted. Sometimes it offered skills and crafts, music, language, legends; and sometimes it offered only sorrow and degradation. Invading samurai introduced the Japanese brand of feudalism; a Mongol horde overran the islands briefly during the Kublai Khan conquests and carried off prisoners to be slaves; and for five centuries Chinese civilization was the Ryukyuan model after the islands had become a tributary of the Middle Kingdom. After Japan decided on a policy of strict isolation, it used the Ryukyus as its chief contact with the outer world; the United States, in turn, employed Okinawa during the time of Commodore Perry as a lever to prise open the closed doors of Japan. Less than a century later, the Ryukyus, still desiring only a quiet life, became the last and bloodiest battlefield of the Second World War.

How did it all start? The creation myth of which I have given a brief account earlier was not actually written down until the mid-seventeenth century, in a more elaborate version that tells us that the gods first created the world by carting stone, sand, and earth to the small island of Kudaka, then planted trees and other growing things there, and finally brought to life a divine child, Tenteishi. The dynasty he founded lasted nearly eighteen thousand years, during which time the other islands were created.

🏯 ISLES OF DIPLOMACY

Curious to know whether modern archaeology has found any evidence to substantiate the Kudaka myth, I learned that the oldest artifacts so far excavated there do not apparently go any further back than the eighth century A.D. On Chinen Peninsula, however, in southern Okinawa, a radio-carbon sampling taken midway down through an ancient midden has revealed material dating as far back as the middle of the second millennium B.C., while an even older settlement has been located near Naha.

But this is far from being the beginning of the story, for geologists tell us that as far back as five or six hundred thousand years ago, there was a land bridge between the Ryukyus and the Asian mainland. During the succeeding geological ages, other land bridges appeared and disappeared, the last occurring about two hundred thousand years ago and continuing for about fifty thousand years, after which the island chain was submerged again except for its highest mountain tops. Then, as eons passed, the waters sank and more solid ground reappeared. There is no reason to suppose that at least as far back as the existence of the last land bridge, human beings, as well as wild beasts, from the Asian mainland did not make use of it.

And indeed there is good evidence to support this supposition. Shell mounds have been found suggesting that there were men leading a stoneage existence on the terraced hills of Okinawa, which appeared after the subsidence of the ocean. From a shell mound in central Okinawa there comes a chipped stone axe, and from other sites in the vicinity polished axes. Even more conclusive evidence is a scrap of a human skull, which, in the opinion of the Japanese geologist who discovered it, may be as old as two hundred thousand years. A great deal more work will have to be done, of course,

OKINAWA 🛕

before any coherent story can be told about the people who lived in the Ryukyus that long ago and about the kind of life that they led. But the presence of stone hammers and adzes and the virtual absence of arrowheads appear to offer conclusive proof that they used traps to catch the wild pigs that they ate.

It is all, to be sure, conjecture, and perhaps must remain so. Even the first contacts in the present era between Okinawans and other peoples are clouded by the mists of unwritten history, but there seems little doubt that the natives of the Ryukyus shared, at least to a certain extent, the same ethnic background as the Chinese and Japanese and Koreans.

In the third century A.D. (and this too is conjecture), migrants are thought to have come out of Korea into Kyushu, continuing on into both Honshu to the north and the northern Ryukyus. It is these people who are believed to have imported the Japanese language into the islands, and the scant evidence that has so far been uncovered suggests also that they imported a new life-style: they lived not in the high terraced hills but by the sea, and they employed tools made of seashells. Dates, as I have said, must, at least for the time being, remain speculative, and scholars of the subject are by no means in agreement. One student of the Japanese language has reckoned that the linguistic separation between Okinawa and Kyoto occured around the year, A.D. 500 after which the Ryukyuan islands continued to develop their own distinct language groups.

Equally tenuous as the early contacts with Japan were those with China, for Okinawa itself possessed no ancient written history while Chinese annals do indeed refer to Liu Ch'iu but with an inconsistency that makes modern scholars uncertain whether the characters refer to Okinawa or Taiwan or both. Chinese coins dating from the

ISLES OF DIPLOMACY

third century B.C. have been found in Okinawa, which suggests the possibility of contact between the two peoples at least as long ago as that, although obviously the contacts may have been so brief as to be virtually meaningless, or the coins may have been brought by later visitors. Through early Chinese history there does indeed run a tenuous thread that speaks of Liu Ch'iu as the land of eternal youth and of the happy immortals, and conjecture has been made that the Chinese sent their first expedition to learn the secrets of happy Ryukyuan immortality as early as 219 B.C. Two more Chinese expeditions are said to have come to the islands in the early seventh century A.D.

The earliest written annals of Okinawan history go back no further than the beginning of the fifteenth century, but clearly by that time there had been prolonged and effective contact with both mainland China and the Japanese islands, and clearly by that time also the native Okinawan kingdom with its fairly well-defined feudal society was already well established. Some historians assert that this society was the result of Japanese infiltration; and dates as early as the eighth century have been given for the first new immigrations from Japan; historians who see the Japanese as the progenitors of Ryukyuan feudal society generally associate that event with samurai quarrels on the home islands.

The point long debated is whether the Japanese who went to Okinawa were from the Taira clan or the Minamoto clan, which clashed at the Battle of Dannoura, on the Inland Sea, in 1185, with the Minamotos emerging victorious. Professor Shunzo Sakamaki states the case for the Tairas in an article in the *Journal of Asian Studies* (XXVII Nov. 67), writing that "the legend about [Minamoto] Tametomo coming to Okinawa and siring a son who founded the first royal Ryukyuan dynasty is pure fantasy ..." He goes on to point out that "the very name 'Taira' became common in many parts of Ryukyu, both as a place-name and as a surname, and the character for 'Taira' appears in numerous compound names," and concludes by saying: "This gap in our knowledge we are trying to fill in with certain conjectures or hypotheses, such as that after the Battle of Dannoura in the year 1185 sizable contingents of the defeated Heike [Taira] forces fled to and settled in Ryukyu, bringing with them considerable wealth, energy, and knowlege, and that they established the first royal dynasty in Ryukyu ..."

Did Tametomo marry the daughter of an Okinawan lord and sire a son who was to become the great King Shunten? So legend insists, although there exists not a scrap of historical proof. What does appear to be fairly well authenticated is that this was a time of constant internal strife in the Ryukyus (Okinawa alone has more than 135 fortified castle sites) and that central authority was not established until 1429, when the lords, or *anji*, pledged their loyalty to King Shō Hashi.

By that time Okinawa was, in a sense, an amalgam in miniature of Chinese and Japanese civilizations. Recognizing Chinese political authority, Okinawa was already paying tribute to the Middle Kingdom (and continued to do so until 1874), a tribute that offered Okinawa various trade advantages without interfering with royal hegemony. In return, China conferred upon Okinawa a system of writing, a predilection for Confucianism that influenced the native religion and provided the basis for a bureaucracy by examination resembling China's, and the yearly almanac that played so important a role in Okinawan daily life. From China too came building methods, styles of dress, and certain new foods. Innovations also made

ISLES OF DIPLOMACY

their way into Okinawa from Japan, although for several centuries Chinese influence remained predominant.

Until the Japanese invasion occurred in the early seventeenth century, Okinawa pretty much followed its own political way, paying tribute to the Chinese, accepting the gifts of Chinese civilization in return, and attempting to consolidate its kingdom, with the anji, often against their will, accepting a supreme ruler. This movement gained impetus at the beginning of the fifteenth century, when Hashi, the anji of Sashiki, emerged from obscurity to engage and defeat the then reigning king, a weakling and, according to legend, an alcoholic. Imbued with Confucian ideals, Hashi put his father on the throne and established his capital at Shuri. Upon his father's death in 1421, Hashi ascended the throne himself, accepting from China the family name of Shō. Within eight years he had unified his kingdom by defeating two rival Okinawan monarchs but found that, although the anji pledged him their loyalty, they still maintained their feudal forces—forces that could never be counted on to disobey their lord in favor of their king. Shō Hashi, accordingly, concentrated on foreign trade, permitting those anji whom he considered well-disposed toward him to share in the profits. It was during this period, and in part as a result of this foreign trade, that the techniques for tie-dye kasuri weaving and stencil dyeing of bingata reached their highest development.

Upon the death of Shō Hashi there followed the familiar dynastic squabbles, from which the dead king's seventh son, Taikyu, emerged victorious. Under his reign, trade increased with both the countries of Southeast Asia and Japan, and Japanese Buddhism became more firmly entrenched at court as the king fell increasingly under the sway of Japanese priests. The monarch's father-in-law, Gosa-

OKINAWA

maru, saw to the erection of Nakagusuku Castle (which continues to be one of Okinawa's chief tourist attractions) and then, just after the castle was completed, found himself obliged to vindicate his honor by committing ritual suicide. His enemies had persuaded the king that Gosamaru was acting as a traitor.

A new dynasty began shortly thereafter when Taikyu's son and all his family were slaughtered and the former royal treasurer, Kanemaro, ascended to the throne in 1470. He took the name of Shō En and founded a dynasty that was to endure for more than four centuries, despite the fact that immediately upon his death its future looked very uncertain. His brother Seni had succeeded him, but Shō En's second wife, now a widow, and a young and ambitious widow at that, determined that her son should follow his father on the throne. What ensued offers ample proof of the power of the nuru in those early days, when the dynastic position of women in Okinawa was far more reminiscent of China than of Japan at that period.

Shortly after the dowager queen discussed the matter of the succession with the chief nuru of the court (who happened to be a daughter of the late King Shō En by his first wife), the nuru had a vision which impelled her to request an audience with the new monarch. Shō Seni, supposing that she desired to congratulate him on his accession to the throne, granted her request, whereupon she announced to all the assembled court that she had received divine instructions that the young prince sitting beside the king should be ruler in the king's place. Shō Seni reigned for less than six months; upon his abdication, Shō Shin, then fourteen years old, became monarch of Okinawa.

As it turned out, the dowager queen and the chief nuru served

ISLES OF DIPLOMACY

their country better than they knew, for Shō Shin was destined to become the Ryukyus' most powerful sovereign and the islands attained the peak of their prosperity during his long reign. The many laws that he promulgated demonstrate what an apt pupil of China Okinawa had become and suggest that Shō Shin was not averse to adopting some of the oppressive measures found in feudal Japan as well as initiating some of his own that were later, in turn, to be adopted by the Japanese.

From the point of view of domestic security, Shō Shin's greatest accomplishment was to put an end to the military power of the anji. They and their followers were forbidden to wear swords, and in fact all weapons were required to be deposited in Shuri, the capital. The king then demanded that all anji, with their families and their most important dependants, assume permanent residence in Shuri. This, from the point of view of the central government, had a number of desirable consequences: it kept the anji effectively under the eye of the king, and it enabled him to benefit from their estates. These were managed by a kind of agent, and the anji were allowed to receive some of the revenue but most went to the monarch, who in turn granted stipends to the lords. The anji were also permitted to engage in foreign trade, which apparently included smuggling and dealing with Japanese pirates, a commerce from which many reaped large profits.

The residence of the anji in Shuri made the capital a more cosmopolitan city, permitting them at the same time to benefit from the capital's cultural and social activities. The anji, further, were classified in a series of ranks and grades ostensibly patterned after China, with competitive examinations such as those used by the Chinese bureaucracy, although the closer a man stood in blood

OKINAWA

relation to the monarch the better his chances were of coming out well in the examinations.

These benefits, however, accrued only to the lords. Other classes found themselves strictly controlled in such matters as the kind of work they could do, the kind of house they could live in, the kind of clothes they could wear, and whether or not they might move from one locality to another. The lowest classes were not even permitted to use footwear or umbrellas. They were closely restricted serfs and remained so throughout the years of the dynasty that was founded by Shō En and given its character by Shō Shin. At the same time, it should be noted that they probably fared no worse than peasants in other parts of contemporary Asia, or, for that matter, in other parts of the world.

Shuri itself, naturally enough, hummed with activity. Suitable houses for the anji and their large establishments had to be erected, and the palace area had to be made continually more imposing. In the first year of the sixteenth century construction began on the royal tombs, and in 1527 the famous Shurei no Mon (Gate of Courtesy) was put up. Of the new Buddhist temples Enkakuji, became the best known in the kingdom; another was built on a small island in the capital's Enkan Pond to house a volume of the sutras presented to the monarch of Okinawa by the monarch of Korea, although Buddhism itself did not become widespread. The nuru system grew more firmly established as a national hierarchy, following the custom that the chief priestess of the state be either an elder sister or daughter of the ruler.

While acknowledging with elaborate ceremonial its cultural indebtedness to China and the pleasant fact that the great Middle Kingdom apparently had no territorial designs on the Ryukyus,

ISLES OF DIPLOMACY

Okinawa felt rather different about Japan, with which it maintained a somewhat nervous relationship. Where China was regarded as a benign and well-meaning parent, Japan loomed in Okinawan eyes as a more enigmatic figure—a figure that might at any moment make unacceptable demands.

That is precisely what happened in 1592, when Toyotomi Hideyoshi invaded Korea: Japan required Okinawan assistance. Okinawa not only refused, it informed China of Japan's intention. Hideyoshi was defeated in Korea, but this did not discourage the Japanese shogunate from pursuing its intention of punishing Okinawan impertinence. Nearly two decades after Hideyoshi's ill-fated expedition, the daimyo of Satsuma (in southern Kyushu), which had for many years claimed title to the Ryukyuan Islands, sent a force of three thousand well-armed warriors to Okinawa. They had little difficulty in conquering the kingdom and capturing its king, who was taken prisoner to Kagoshima and kept there in exile for two years.

While the Okinawan refusal to cooperate with Japan in the Korean adventure offered an immediate reason for this invasion, there were other, and longer-standing, contributing factors. One was Okinawa's gradual encroachment on islands to the north, islands that the Satsuma daimiate regarded as indisputably part of its territory; another was Okinawa's enviable prosperity as a trading nation; still a third was the shogunate's uneasiness over militant Christianity, which began in 1549 with the appearance in Kagoshima of Francis Xavier and ended, temporarily, with the first expulsion by edict in 1610; and yet a fourth may have been the fact that the shogun liked to keep his samurai occupied at home.

In any case, Japan did not return the captured king until Okinawa

OKINAWA

agreed to recognize Satsuma suzerainty and to pay an annual tribute of rice. The unfortunate Ryukyuan monarch was so shamed by his capture and imprisonment that he asked not to be buried with his ancestors in the royal tombs but rather to have his body tucked modestly away on a cliff below Urasoe Castle.

Japan's two initial demands, as might have been anticipated, soon burgeoned. Satsuma annexed the northern Ryukyuan islands directly, and in the Okinawan capital, although Japan did not attempt to assume control, it stationed a number of agents. Okinawa, fearful that its new relations with Japan might mean a rupture with China, was relieved to find that the two mighty nations were apparently content to use Shuri as a kind of exchange post. The relief was, however, only temporary, for it was soon obvious that Japan, while ostensibly agreeing to the maintenance of trade between Shuri and Peking, intended to take for itself all the profits of that trade. After 1637, when the shogunate closed the doors of Japan to all outside commerce, the Satsuma daimiate grew rich smuggling in goods from Okinawa, while the Okinawans themselves grew poorer and poorer.

They also fell increasingly under Japanese influence. Idle aristocrats for example, soon became infatuated with the tea ceremony, which, since it requires a number of utensils, gave impetus to the development of Okinawa's pottery industry. The growing Japanese influence during the years that followed increased Okinawan interest in other folk crafts as well as in Japanese drama and temple architecture. Of greater cultural impact on the kingdom was Japanese hostility to the nuru system, resulting in a gradual diminution of the importance of women in Okinawan political life, a shift that was highly agreeable to the now Japanese-trained, Confucian-

ISLES OF DIPLOMACY

minded, and (as some might say today) male-chauvinist officials of the court. At the same time, of great economic importance was the introduction into Okinawa of sweet potatoes and sugarcane from China, for these hardy crops became the mainstay of the typhoon-haunted islands and also the chief agricultural products smuggled into Japan after the closed-door policy came into effect.

Between the Satsuma invasion of 1609 and outright Japanese annexation in 1879, Okinawan life idled along—its monarchs exercising little real power, its nobility and gentry (about a quarter of the population) drifting lazily into poverty, its nuru losing many of their ancient high prerogatives, and its commoners going on as before—tightly regimented, hardworking, and ill rewarded. Many historians see in these centuries of lethargy the formation of the pliant Ryukyuan character that was commented on so frequently by early Western visitors to the islands. Torn between their ancient allegiance to China and their newer subordination to Japan, forced to live as amicably as they could under the shadow of the two great powers, the Ryukyuans developed those qualities of easygoing acquiescence and suppleness of character that enabled them, in the Japanese phrase, to bend with the wind no matter how strong it blew and no matter what direction it happened to be blowing from—China or Japan, Europe or America.

The West entered very late onto the Okinawan scene: not, in fact, until the early nineteenth century, after John McLeod, a surgeon aboard the *Alceste*, which had brought Lord Amherst to China on a special mission, published his *Narrative of a Voyage in His Majesty's late ship Alceste*, which was followed a year later by Basil Hall, captain of the sloop *Lyra*, who broke into print with *An Account of a Voyage of Discovery to the West Coast of Corea and the*

OKINAWA

Great Loo-Choo Island. It was the latter that, despite its cumbersome title, here abridged, most effectively captured the imagination of the West, bringing to the Ryukyuans an attention they did not desire and only hastening the day when Japan would feel herself compelled to rationalize her ambiguous relations with Okinawa by simply making the islands part of her empire.

When Hall's very laudatory book appeared, that day was still well over half a century off, but by the time the next explorer-writer of consequence appeared along the Okinawan coast the bell could be heard distantly beginning to toll the end of the kingdom's nominal independence. The new intruder was a dour, pompous man of sixty, a career naval officer who had attained the honorary rank of commodore and who had been sent by his government to prise open the closed doors of Japan, for his government ruled a young and vigorous nation that badly wanted trading partners at a time when most of the world's ports were controlled by European powers. He was Matthew Calbraith Perry, of Kingston, Rhode Island.

He had commanded America's first steam warship, he had been to Africa to help suppress the slave trade, he had taken part in the war with Mexico, and now, on May 26, 1853, he found himself in command of five American ships anchored just outside Shuri's Tomari Port. Perry was on his way to Japan, a country so secluded from the rest of the world that Perry's own government did not know Japan possessed two rulers, the emperor in Kyoto and the shogun, sometimes translated tycoon, in Tokyo (then called Edo). A few years later, the President of the United States was to speak of "His Imperial Majesty the Tycoon."

On the basis of the scanty information available to him, Perry

ISLES OF DIPLOMACY

had come to the conclusion that Okinawa offered the best port in the vicinity of Japan for an initial rendezvous. He knew, of course, from his reading, that the Ryukyuans were not a bellicose people and that they did not in fact even bear arms, a factor of importance to an officer venturing into unknown territory.

Shortly after Perry arrived, a rowboat pulled up alongside his flagship and a European climbed aboard. This, it turned out, was Dr. Bernard J. Bettelheim, a physician and a converted Jew who had been sent to Okinawa by a missionary society in 1846. During the years, he had failed miserably in his mission, a fact that may well have embittered him, with the result that by the time of Perry's arrival he was cordially disliked by the islanders. He could not in any case ever have been very popular, for any Okinawan found by a member of the Japanese police to have shown interest in Christianity would have been summarily punished, perhaps executed. Okinawan hostility to Bettelheim was apparently reciprocated, and it may well have been he who initially prejudiced Perry against the Ryukyuans, in particular the aristocrats, whom the American commodore characterized in his official account as sly and undependable. Or it may have been the fact that Perry, who habitually looked as though he had been assailed by some highly offensive odor, was not a man to bring out the best in people, even gentle and courteous Okinawans.

He began his intrusive visit by refusing to meet any Ryukyuans save the highest dignitaries. When the regent finally came aboard, Perry announced succinctly that he would visit the royal palace on 6 June for an audience with the king. The regent's attempts to dissuade him failed, and accordingly, on the announced morning, the Americans disembarked and headed for Shuri Castle. In the grand

OKINAWA

march were two bands, three companies of marines, and the ships' officers; the commodore himself was carried in a freshly made palanquin painted red and blue. As the procession approached the castle, the regent, Prince Shō Jun, sought to divert it to the palace of the crown prince, but on Perry's orders the Americans continued straight up the hill through the Gate of Courtesy to the main doors of the castle. These they found locked.

Anticipating that a man as obdurate as Perry might well order the doors to be shot open, the regent hastily sent a man around through a side gate to unlock them. The commodore, followed by his officers, marched into the audience hall only to find it as empty of royalty as it was of preparations for a state visit of the sort that Perry had obviously envisaged. The unwelcome guests seated themselves and for the next hour stared in stony silence at the regent and his officers. When, at last, the regent suggested that they all repair to the regent's mansion for some refreshments, even Perry was amenable. He was pleasantly surprised by the twelve-course Chinese-style banquet that was waiting for him and his men.

During the first week, a party of the visiting Americans made a six-day tour of the island. They were looking for coal deposits, for ports that might be of future use, and for general information about Okinawa and Okinawans. Bayard Taylor, a famous writer and journalist of the day who is probably best known now for his translation of Goethe's *Faust*, was a member of the expedition, and his account of it, published in Perry's official narrative, offers a fascinating picture of island life at mid-century, only a few years before Japanese annexation was to alter it irreparably.

It was from Naha that Perry launched his two journeys to Japan, presenting a letter from President Fillmore to shogunate officials

ISLES OF DIPLOMACY

at Uraga on the first voyage and on the second taking his famous "black ships" into Edo Bay. On March 31, 1854, Perry succeeded in concluding the first treaty between the United States and Japan. He had also pressured the Okinawan government into signing a compact which guaranteed cooperation with all American ships that might call at the Ryukyus, but now that Japan herself was opened to American trade, the value of Okinawan ports was greatly diminished.

Perry's visit was not, however, without consequences in Ryukyuan life. For one thing, to universal relief, he took Dr. Bettelheim away. For another, his visit furnished further evidence of increasing Western interest in the Far East and made Japan more apprehensive than before about the possibility of the Chinese reaching an agreement with a Western power that would give them sovereignty over the Ryukyus.

To frustrate any likelihood of this, Japan announced to the world in 1872 that the kingdom of Okinawa was now a *han*, that is to say, a feudal domain within the Japanese empire. The title of the last Okinawan monarch, Shō Tai, was changed to "king of the Ryukyuan Han." For seven years Shō Tai contrived to avert outright incorporation into the empire, but finally in 1879 he was carried off to Tokyo, while Okinawa and all the islands south of it were reclassified as a *ken*, a prefecture. As Shō Tai sailed away, a garrison of Japanese soldiers occupied his castle.

Along with political change went drastic and unprecedented changes in a social structure that had evolved and crystalized over many centuries. Since the mass of the people were illiterate and of course unfamiliar with modern Japanese (despite a common background somewhere in the distant past), Tokyo decided that the best

OKINAWA

way to inaugurate the Japanization process was through education. In 1879, there were only thirty schools in the entire prefecture, and these were attended solely by children of nobles. A little more than a decade later, seventy-one additional schools had been established and three years of elementary education had been made compulsory, but only about 15 percent of school-age children attended: tuition, although cheap was still more than peasants could afford. Finally, in 1908, a system of free compulsory education was established.

When the imperial government's attempt to put an end to the rigid Okinawan class system met with strong opposition, Tokyo simply replaced those nobles who held key positions with men from Japan proper. The most overwhelming change, one which affected the mass of the people, was the abolition of communal land holdings. This system, which had existed since long before recorded history, is far too complex for me to attempt any detailed exposition of it. Briefly, however, some three quarters of Ryukyuan arable land was owned communally by the villages, the rest being held by the royal family, the anji, and the nuru; provision was made for occasional redistribution of the land, first to groups of families and then to individual households; taxes, usually in the form of agricultural products or textiles, were imposed not on individuals but on families or groups of families; if one household could not pay its taxes, then other households within the family group would make up the difference; maintenance and inheritance of land were also determined by the communal system.

Between 1899 and 1903, Japan attempted to legislate communal land tenure out of existence, substituting the Japanese system of private property, responsibility, taxation and inheritance. In view of the fact that this reform would inevitably change the whole way

ISLES OF DIPLOMACY

of Okinawan life, it was at first strongly resisted by traditionally conservative villagers, although eventually, in most places, the new masters of the Ryukyus were to have their way. Even today, however, in a couple of the smaller islands, the communal system still prevails.

Another problem that the Japanese tried to solve in those years between annexation and war was overpopulation. Officials sought to persuade residents of the main island to migrate to smaller islands such as Yaeyama and Miyako, but most Okinawans felt they would just as soon stay where they were. Nor did Japanese attempts to induce Ryukyuans to emigrate to other parts of the world meet with overwhelming success. In 1899 the first contingent of Okinawans went to Hawaii to work on the sugarcane plantations: in all, that contingent numbered twenty-seven intrepid souls. As the years passed, however, other Okinawans followed, not only to Hawaii but to mainland America as well, to Taiwan and the Philippines. By 1907 there were some ten thousand Ryukyuans resident abroad.

Soon, now, Japan was to embark upon her dream, or her nightmare, of armed conquest, an adventure in which Okinawans were destined to play their unavoidable and tragic role. Having fought China and won, then having fought Russia and won, Japan could foresee no limit to her future imperial boundaries, at least upon the Asian mainland and in the islands of the Pacific. Long-term preparations were initiated, and soon the military establishment had edged its way into control of civilian life. Ryukyuans, who had frequently felt themselves treated as second-class subjects of the emperor, were now commanded to prepare to give their lives for the greater glory of his empire. One middle-aged Naha businessman

OKINAWA 🎎

told me one day, "When I was a boy, if anybody asked me what I wanted to be when I grew up, I would always answer, 'A soldier.' That was the answer we all gave at the time."

During the first months of the war, the news was invigorating: Japanese troops were victorious wherever they went, and Ryukyuans shared in the general elation. They felt no premonition of impending disaster. But as the war wore on, as American troops began retaking island after island, as the energy moved ever closer toward Japan herself, there came a growing feeling of unease and apprehension, a feeling that was not abated when Okinawans saw high Japanese officials on the island send their families back home. Every available Ryukyuan was conscripted; age limits were extended at both ends of the scale; those who were held unfit for military duty were drafted into a work force. Food grew as scarce as in the home islands, perhaps even scarcer. Old women worked hard building bomb shelters that all too soon were seen to be wholly useless.

On October 10, 1944, American carrier-based planes made more than a thousand strikes over the city of Naha and the airfields and docks. The city was ninety percent destroyed. Despite reassurances by the Japanese military, Okinawans could no longer doubt that they were destined to bear the first brunt of the Allied attack on Japan. The onslaught began in earnest the following March, with the invasion of the islands of Kerama; then, on the first day of April, more than thirteen hundred Allied vessels pulled up at the eight-mile stretch of beach at Toguchi, on Okinawa, and before nightfall over sixty thousand troops had landed virtually unopposed.

The opposition came later—the battle for Okinawa had begun, and before it ended on June 21 the conquered island lay in ruins. During the fighting, some twelve thousand Allied troops were

ISLES OF DIPLOMACY

killed and another thirty-seven thousand wounded; on the Japanese side, casualty reports gave no significant number of wounded, but more than ninety thousand died. Immediately after the war, deaths of Okinawan civilians were estimated to number about forty-seven thousand. Later, some historians upped that figure to over two hundred thousand.

Those who survived were for a time hardly aware of having done so. They had no houses to live in, no food to eat, no doctors to cleanse their wounds or treat their battle-induced illnesses. Never had they seen so many lice, lice that infested their matted hair and the seams of their unwashed rags of clothing; with horror they watched maggots crawling in and out of their putrifying wounds. American broadcasts and leaflets dropped by American planes promised safety to civilians and to soldiers who would lay down their arms; but had not the Japanese military repeatedly said that the invading barbarians would torture and kill all whom they captured? Nevertheless, according to many military observers, Okinawans seemed far readier to surrender than other Japanese. Perhaps the jingoism of state Shinto had never meant very much to the Ryukyuan islanders.

The quarter-century of American occupation that followed was not an unmixed success. It brought in dollars, to be sure, at a time when dollars were highly regarded in the world, but it also brought in the incompetence, the inhumanity, and the corrupting influence of a military occupation.

Considering the tremendous sacrifices it had made to win Okinawa, the United States felt justified in holding on to it. Further, the Americans desired to maintain a presence in the Far East, and Okinawa was one of the obvious places in which to maintain it.

OKINAWA 🏯

But for career military men, the devastated Ryukyuan dumping ground was one of the least desirable of all postwar assignments. Commanding officers were changed so frequently they never had a chance to become acquainted with the problems that needed to be solved. Discipline on the side of the occupying forces was weak; morale on both sides was low.

Then, in 1949, came a typhoon, ironically named Gloria, that eventually brought an American team to Okinawa to investigate the widespread destruction the storm had left behind. More shocking than the damage itself, the team reported, was the inaction of the military administration. A shake-up followed that brought in new officers with plans for the rehabilitation of the island as well as for permanent bases. The strategic importance of Okinawa was demonstrated the following year, when the United Nations took "police action" in Korea. The result was a huge build-up of American military installations in Okinawa.

But the Okinawans themselves were far from satisfied. While they appreciated the measure of prosperity that was coming their way as a result of the continuing American occupation, they were beginning to feel once again like a forgotten people. Majority sentiment favored reversion to Japan. In 1951 a petition to that effect was presented at the San Francisco Peace Conference, and from then on Okinawans agitated more and more strenuously for eventual return. They saw that Japan itself had achieved autonomy and was already building up its economy, while they themselves were ruled by the United States, although they were not American citizens nor were they citizens of Japan, as they had been before the war.

Then, in June, 1961, came good news: Prime Minister Hayato

⛩ ISLES OF DIPLOMACY

Ikeda of Japan and President John F. Kennedy of the United States had an exchange of views in which they agreed that Japan maintained residual sovereignty in Okinawa and the southern Ryukyus. (The Amami Islands had reverted some years back to Japan.) In March, 1962, President Kennedy announced: "The Ryukyu Islands are a part of the Japanese territory." But still the long desired reversion did not materialize. In August, 1965, Prime Minister Sato said that the postwar period could not end "unless and until the reversion of Okinawa to the motherland is realized."

And finally, on May 15, 1972, shortly before Sato retired from public life, Okinawa became once again a Japanese prefecture. It has rejoined the mother land; it is an integral part of one of the most economically prosperous and politically peaceful nations in the world. Ryukyuans expect that the motherland will do all it can to compensate for the horrors of war and the long years of occupation. In that case, Okinawa, with its agreeable climate and its even more agreeable people, may well turn into one of the most popular places in the world for people to come who want to breathe clean air, wander across simple countryside, and bathe in clear water. We who have learned to love Okinawa can only hope that success will not spoil it.

92-94. *Nakagusuku Castle: far left*, tomb of Gosamaru, builder of the castle; *left*, "Banner Rock," near Nakagusuku, named by the Perry expedition; *previous page*, the famous archway, built without a keystone.

96. *An Okinawan prince* and his two sons, were portrayed in 1816 by a British artist aboard H.M.S. *Lyra*.

◀95. *The lower terrace* of the castle was erected in the fifteenth century to guard Shuri Castle against attacks from the north.

97. *A courtyard* of Chinen Castle: the kings of Okinawa always stopped here on their sacred tours of the Chinen Peninsula.

98-100. *Machinato* was once Okinawa's chief port: *far left*, a sketch of the promontory above the port made by one of Commodore Perry's explorers in 1863, and *left*, one of "Banner Rock"; *below*, United States military warehouses, stretching for miles near Machinato.

101-102. *Two kings*: Shō Nei, shamed by his defeat at the hands of the Japanese in 1609, asked to be buried in the hillside beneath Urasoe Castle (*below*); *bottom*, a shrine on Chinen Peninsula dedicated to Shō Hashi, the remarkable ruler who reunited the country in 1429.

103-104. *Shuri Castle,* the ancient home of Okinawa's kings, was completely destroyed during the Second World War, although vestiges of its former glory remain or have been restored. *Left,* Ryutan pond, the center of the royal garden; *below,* a shrine put up originally to house a Buddhist sutra presented by Korea's king was recently rebuilt.

105-107. *Royal remains*: shrine just outside Shuri Castle was the gateway to the sacred grove of the chief priestess (*above*); road paved with stones (*right*) led from the castle to the royal villa at Aza-Maji, now a part of East Naha; *below*, remains of the royal tombs of the second Shō dynasty.

◀108. *Shurei no Mon,* the Gate of Courtesy (*previous page*), is the appropriate symbol of the courteous Ryukyuan people.

109-110. *The torii* ("gateway," *above left*) that leads to Nami-no-ue, destroyed during the war and rebuilt, is once again the prefecture's chief shrine. A Buddhist temple, Gokokuji (*above*), stands beside Nami-no-ue; this gateway too was destroyed during the war and a faithful copy re-erected in its place.

111-116. *Ryukyuan faces* (*clockwise from above*): an older woman bearing her burden in the traditional way; a tourist guide wearing a Taiwanese hat; two friends smiling in the rain; a couple of boys playing cards on the sidewalk; the proprietor of a small scarf shop; three boys discovered in their secret hiding place.

117. *The University of the Ryukyus*, erected with American funds in 1950, stands on the site of the vanished Shuri Castle.

118. *The Okinawa Prefecture Museum* (*opposite center*), in Shuri, was constructed in 1966, also largely with American backing.

119. *The highway* between Naha and Kadena (*opposite below*), although four- and six-lane, is often jammed with bumper-to-bumper traffic.

120. *The international cemetery* (*right*), near Tomari Port: six of Commodore Perry's men lie buried here.

121. *The bars* on Kosa Center Street (*below*) are popular with off-duty American military personnel.

122-123. *Stone monuments* (*above*) mark the spots where Lieutenant General Buckner, commanding the 10th U. S. Army, and Ernie Pyle, popular war correspondent, were killed during the Battle of Okinawa.

124-125. *Japanese forces* made their headquarters in underground tunnels (*below*). Both Vice Admiral Ota and Lieutenant General Ushijima committed suicide when they realized defeat was inevitable.

126-128. *Mute reminders* of the "bloodiest battlefield": a Japanese coast artillery gun (*above*); Shuri Church, one of the two buildings still standing in Shuri after the bombardment (*above right*); anchor from a Japanese warship (*below*).

129. *The fall of "Conical Hill"* (*overleaf*) led to the crumbling of the entire Japanese defense line and the end of the battle for Okinawa.

THIS BEAUTIFUL WORLD

The Himalayas	Lapland
Palaces of Kyoto	The Greek Islands
Peking	Hong Kong
Gods of Kumano	Angkor Wat
Moscow	Istanbul
Michelangelo	The Road to Holy Mecca
Afghanistan	
Hawaii	Burma
Seoul	The Andes
Goya	New Guinea
The Alps	Marketplaces of the World
The Acropolis	
Vienna	Tokyo
African Animals	Ireland
Thailand	Australia
Yosemite	India
San Francisco	Cherry Blossoms
Bali	Okinawa
Spain	New York
Mexico	London
Imperial Villas of Kyoto	Sri Lanka
	Iran
Journey through Africa	Yugoslavia
	Washington
The Grand Canyon	Rome
California	Brazil
Mongolia	

In preparation

Alaska	Dehli